At a time and season whe
paced world that's revo
enough time to complete and fulfill the dreams and visions that
God has given us, how refreshing it is to pick up a manuscript
that addresses the challenges that confront the passion that
enables us to fulfill our purpose.

Enjoy the Journey allows you a look into the life of Torrey
Phillips, one of God's chosen generals. Get ready to be moved
and motivated by the honesty he reveals in the ups and downs,
the bumps and bruises, and the challenges we all face on this
journey called life. He is a husband, father, pastor, author, and a
preacher of integrity. It is my honor to call him a son in the gospel.

Bishop Joby R. Brady
Before the Foundation
The River Church
Durham, N.C.

Torrey Phillips is best described as a cross between Moses and
Joshua. He possesses the wisdom of Moses and vision of
Joshua, as a focused leader of God's people. I've evaluated his
preparation, prayer life, and progress through the years, and I
know that he's been anointed to minister to this generation.

He is not just my spiritual son, but my biological son as well,
and I'm proud of him and what God is doing through him. I'm
blessed to have witnessed his first book, *Enjoy the Journey*.
Read it and be blessed.

Rev. Dr. T.G. Thompson
Gospel Arena Of Faith Churches, Inc.
Fort Lauderdale, FL

I am ecstatic to be able to finally share with the world its
greatest hidden secret jewel, Pastor Torrey Phillips. Not only is

he an exceptional husband and father, but also, like David, a man after God's own heart. Torrey Phillips is a man on whom God has released an abundance of insight, wisdom, and authority in the Word of God. He is a leader who has distinguished his assignment of equipping believers to handle life's challenges and adversity as triumphs. In his first published book, *Enjoy the Journey*, Pastor Torrey takes the reader on a mental and spiritual trek. Life will never be the same for the reader after reading *Enjoy the Journey*.

Through reading this insightful and captivating work of art, I have been motivated to refrain from accelerating towards the promises of God, and have learned to focus on simply enjoying the unfolding of life. As a result of reading *Enjoy the Journey,* my perception of success has broadened. I understand that success is not measured in quantity, but rather in quality. And although I haven't received the fulfillment of God's promises, every small obstacle and step that I've overcome is a victory meant to be acknowledged. Each time that I persevere should be a time of celebration, no matter how insignificant it may seem.

Pastor Torrey said in *Barren but Blessed*, "sometimes, the closer we get to laying hold of the promises of God, the greater the obstacles. Whenever there have been delays, get ready to break into a song." This is what we need to hear. So many times we have been told to begin to celebrate only when we reach our goal. But imagine what would happen if, as happened to the children of Israel, a promised victory is postponed. We could choose to exist in a stagnating and defeated mental state, and miss out on enjoying the journey of the life that God has given us.

Enjoy the Journey is a publication of Pastor Torrey's struggles in life, while he has aggressively pursued the vision that God birthed in him. It is a diary of many realistic areas where he was oftentimes tested and tried, and, with the grace of God, overcame. My prayers are that through Pastor Torrey's penetrating, keen, animated, and perceptive look into a journey all mankind must travel, each person will be strengthened and empowered to stay the course and finish strong. I know that after reading this testament to God's sovereignty at work in the role of creation, individual purpose, and assignment, you too will be inspired to just do it, and...*Enjoy the Journey!*

Keisha Phillips
Keisha Phillips Ministries, CEO
Gospel of Christ Church
Ft. Lauderdale Fl

Process is not a word I associate only with myself. Process has made me the person I am. There is no way you can journey though this life without coming into contact with process. Process is forward or onward movement. It is married to the journey. Life would not be the same without process. Process is good for you. It helps perfect you if you let it.

Life is all about process. There will never be a great deal of success in anyone's life without process. The things we go through in life equip us for the journey that has been prepared for us by God. Journey means travel from place to place. As we travel from one place to the next, it is important that we get the blessing and the lesson. In the midst of the traveling, we may never really enjoy the journey, because we are so busy trying to get to the destination that we bypass the lesson. And because we are so interested in getting to our destination (the blessing) we never really truly understand the value of the journey. There are always teachable moments in a journey, but you must be open enough to learn. These moments will teach you what no school can teach you. My most life-changing moments have been while I was on the journey. A true, authentic journey will revolutionize your life, so it is important that you enjoy it.

As you go from place to place, you will see that all places are connected together. God knows exactly what he is doing. As these places connect, your destiny will begin to unfold right before your very eyes. If you examine the places you have traveled, mentally, spiritually, socially, emotionally or financially, you will see that you have encountered something different in each place. It is important that you understand that those encounters must not be wasted, but must be filed in the archives of your spirit, so that while you are on this journey called life, you will always have a spiritual file to refer to. Every experience you have ever had, be it good, bad, or ugly, plays a major role in your journey. It is the experiences you have had at each place that help shape your big picture (your vision). Your journey is important. It is where you are tried, tested, proven, and cultivated for the purpose the Lord has for you.

In reading this wonderful book, you will discover that if you make up your mind not to fight the journey but to enjoy it, the journey will squeeze your very best out of you. I challenge you to let each chapter be your compass while you are traveling from faith to faith and glory to glory. You will see that the words penned on each page have been inspired by God. If you grasp the message of *Enjoy the Journey*, you will not only learn the importance of enjoying the journey, but you will discover how to live every day of your life with passion.

Torrey Phillips teaches us in this book that success does not come easily, but is a process. We must be willing to allow God's process to refine us to become who He has destined us to be. And while the process is refining us, we must not compete, compare, or complain. **Let the Journey begin !**

Pastor Ocie Reese
Anointed Word Church
Atlanta, Ga.

Torrey Phillips is one of the most profound voices of our time. In this book, *Enjoy the Journey*, Torrey exposes the pressure of pursuing destiny, and offers solutions to maintain the victory on your way. I highly recommend reading this book

Apostle Amos Benefield
Anointed Word International Church
Fort Lauderdale, Fl.

Pastor Torrey Phillips is not only a young vessel tailor-made for this hour, but he is an author who has managed to masterfully convey practical and insightful wisdom, gleaned from his own personal and spiritual experiences. In his book, *Enjoy the Journey! Living Everyday of Your Life with Passion,* Pastor Phillips offers a refreshing perspective on the journey of life. After reading this book, you will have a greater understanding of the necessity to properly process and celebrate your own personal life's journey, while recognizing the importance of your incremental success. I am excited to write an endorsement for this wonderful book. It is relevant to all ages and is a much-needed work for this season that we are experiencing in Christ Jesus.

Evangelist Nichelle L. Early
Founder & President Break Forth Ministries
ConsultingFounder & Executive Editor,
PreachingWoman.com
Washington, DC

This inspirational book certainly challenges every reader to embrace God's divine choice of travel for our lives. I believe Pastor Torrey Phillips' revelation will inspire everyone to let Patience have her perfect course in Life. *Enjoy the Journey* is life-changing.

Bishop Hurricane Johnson
Changing Your Life Ministry
Fort Lauderdale, Fl.

As a pastor, husband, father, brother, and friend, I have found ***Enjoy the Journey*** to be a valuable tool in directing individuals to live every day of life with passion, despite all of life's challenges.

Pastor Torrey Phillips, inspired by God with vision and purpose, has compiled a unique and simple plan for how to deal with the various aspects of life's journey, and how to get to our final destination with passion and an overall goal in mind.

Pastor Phillips' compilation enlightens, encourages, and inspires the believer to live life passionately, beyond every worldly principality. This book will teach you how not to loose focus on your dreams, and will inspire God's people to keep their eyes on the prize.

Pastor Marc Cooper
Cooper's Temple Upper Room Ministries
Miami, Fl.

Pastor Torrey Phillips had the passion to preach the Gospel of Jesus Christ from the age of twelve years. I had the pleasure to watch as God groomed him in each stage of his ministry first as a youth pastor, then a well-grounded evangelist, to becoming the pastor of one the largest and fastest-growing churches in Fort Lauderdale, Florida. His anointed preaching and humorous teaching of the word of God has healed, saved, and blessed the lives of many people. Pastor Torrey Phillips' life-changing writings in this book will push you to become an extraordinary Christian. When you read this book I promise you that your life will experience the extravagant blessings of God. This book is highly recommended for biblical teaching and training for spiritual growth.

Pastor Junior Thompson
Gospel Arena International Ministry of Miami
Miami, Fl.

Pastor Torrey Phillips, a spiritual son and friend, has written a challenging and thought-provoking book that I am sure will cause its readers to take a long and serious look at themselves— especially those who are trapped in a state of inertia because they are not where they think they ought to be in life, personally or professionally. They have not realized that God's delays are not necessarily denials.

Phillips challenges his readers to accept the fact that life itself is a process. Real success is progressive and not instantaneous. Too many people, pastors included, become discouraged and even depressed about where they are presently, because they see the achievements of others, who, in many instances, may not have the academic, social, or political acumen as they.

Therefore, they develop what Phillips calls "a spirit of comparison." Whenever we begin to compare ourselves and our situations with others, we soon lose appreciation for the blessings that God has given to us. We begin thinking that God is unfair to us and fail to realize that whatever we have is a gift from God. Since everything is a gift from God, we should never covet what God has given someone else. We should live each day being grateful that God has blessed us with another day to fully exercise our gifts in a spirit of excellence.

I have personally known individuals who became caught in the comparison game, became angry, and never gave God their best. They never stopped to ask God the question, "What is your plan for my life? What do you want me to do?" They simply judged their lives by what other had. They judged their church's success by what other churches were doing, or what other pastors claimed the churches were doing. Therefore, they never developed an attitude of gratitude.

Because of the world in which we live, we can all find reasons to complain and be ungrateful. However, it all boils down to our perspective on life. If your perspective is that God is unfair, you will never appreciate what you have or where you are. In fact, you will live a mediocre life, facing each day with distain. However, if your perspective is that God knows exactly what He is doing, where you are going, how and when you will get there, you will live life victoriously and declare with Paul, "Now thanks be to God who always leads us in triumph in Christ" (2 Cor. 2:14).

Whatever lies ahead, trust that God has a plan for your life and "enjoy the journey."

Dr. C. E. Glover
Mount Bethel Baptist Church,
Ft. Lauderdale, Fl.

ENJOY THE JOURNEY

Living every day of your life with passion

Torrey Phillips

Llumina
Christian
Books

ISBN: 978-1-59526-949-2

Printed in the United States of America by Llumina Christian Books

Library of Congress Control Number: 2007909939

DEDICATION/ ACKNOWLEDGEMENT

I firmly believe that Family and Friendship are amazing gifts from God, so I'm grateful to have a rich friendship and relationship with my high school sweet heart, Keisha, thank you for your support.

I'm grateful for my beautiful and brilliant children, all of you represent a unique and special gift from God. Thank you all

I'm grateful to have the support of "the world's greatest church." Your confidence in my leadership, made this book possible. Thank you.

I'm the product of every mentor, teacher, friend and relationship that have ever challenged me beyond my comfort zone

- Dr. T.G Thompson, my father, thank you for speaking into my life and encouraging my ministry. Your teaching and preaching prepared me for this day! Thank you

- Bishop Victor T. Curry, my spiritual covering and mentor, your vision, tenacity and fearless leadership continue to challenge my life and ministry. Thank you

- Dr. C.E. Glover, one of the greatest gifts I've ever met, your love for me, my family and my ministry has encouraged me in ways beyond articulation. Thank you.

- Dr. Ocie Reese, your friendship and model of Leadership/Ministry have had an indelible impact on my life and ministry. Thank you.

- Pastor Marc Cooper, you have been a real brother to me. Thank you.

- Apostle Rob Jones, your prophetic insight prepared me for my destiny. Thank you.

- Pastor Alice Phillips, my mother, I couldn't have asked for a better one. Thank you.

CONTENTS

Foreword   i

Introduction   iii

One   Enjoy the Journey   1

Two   Barren, but Blessed   5

Three   Take the Scenic Route   11

Four   It's Working Together!   17

Five   God Has Not Changed His Mind   21

Six   Undetected Victories   25

Seven   Travel Light   29

Eight   Respect the Process   33

Nine   Are You Ready Yet?   37

Ten   From Start to Finish   43

Eleven   Lord, Show Me Your Plan   49

Twelve   Get Your Foot Off the Brakes   55

Thirteen   Don't Forget Your Keys   59

FOREWORD

While there are many complex matters to address in this life, Jesus gave us the most profound and fundamental focus when He expresses His purpose "... I am come that they might have life, and that they might have it more abundantly." (John 10:10b). We all face the daily struggle to succeed, to accomplish and produce, but the common thread that should be apparent for us all is that of a bountiful, lavish, rich life - God's kind of life, to have that life and to have it more abundantly.

In this manuscript we gain the privilege of stepping back to take inventory of our life journey. Torrey Phillips has provided an exceptional opportunity to bring the zest and passion that makes life worth living back to our lives. Oftentimes we find ourselves in a rut and just barely getting from one day to the next but this project, if read with introspection, will navigate you through that wilderness of a mere existence to the life that we were meant to have and enjoy.

I challenge you to enter these pages with the expectation of a radical heart change; to trust this book to refocus your life view, to acquire the view of the Master and see all of life-both the triumphs and the trials-as something to treasure and savor. I invite you to enter these pages with childlike anticipation and allow this work to reposition your heart and your life for the abundance that we so desperately long for and He so faithfully has provided.

Bishop Victor T. Curry, D. Min., D. Div.
Senior Pastor/Teacher
New Birth Baptist Church Cathedral of Faith International

INTRODUCTION

Dear Reader,

Welcome! I'm sure that, whoever you are, you want to enjoy a life filled and fueled with passion, and as a fellow traveler on the incredible journey called Life, I can tell you that it's imperative to seek God's heart for insight and instructions. I believe that this book will provide valuable inspiration for achieving your goals.

Enjoying life has a lot to do with how passionate one is about it, and so periodically, I look at my life to see whether I'm enduring or enjoying it.

Here are some questions I ask myself:

- What makes me happy?
- What makes me scared?
- What are my hopes?
- What gives me inspiration?
- What is it about this person that attracts me to them?
- What is it about this career that I've stop here?
- What is it about this church that keeps me coming?
- What is it about this college that I just love?

These questions will help you define the quality of your life and could show you why you have not been enjoying the journey.

The life that you're living now and your answers to these questions hint to where you're headed in the future. Life is a journey. Every day is a little bit different from the next. Every day, your answers may change. And that's cool, too.

- Priorities change
- Desires change
- Goals change
- Dreams change

And the way we go about achieving what makes us happy changes. That's the way it should be. But the answers to these questions give you an idea of where you are right now and where you're headed.

Here are three simple steps to getting the most out of this book:

- read each page
- take a few minutes to reflect on what you've learned
- in a journal or notebook, write down the insight you've gained

Above all, act upon what you read; after all, what good is inspiration if it's not backed up by action?

Thank you for allowing me to share my heart with you. I pray you find something in these pages that moves you in a special way.

—Torrey Phillips

I AM COME THAT THEY
MIGHT HAVE LIFE,
AND THAT THEY,
MIGHT HAVE *IT* MORE ABUNDANTLY
(JOHN 10:10b)

ONE

ENJOY THE JOURNEY

Take this for the journey:

Faith honors God and God honors faith.
~ Bishop Victor T. Curry ~

Success is never a destination. It's a journey.
~ Satenig St. Marie ~

When I am anxious, it is because I am living in the future. When
I am depressed, it is because I am living in the past.

Do not follow where the path may lead.
Go instead where there is no path, and leave a trail.
~ Author Unknown ~

God inspired this book in a season of frustration and delay. I was living in the unfolding of God's plan for my life, but what he had in store for me had not come to fruition. When promises linger unfulfilled, some individuals become so overwhelmed by the absence of what they think they should have or where they think they should be, that they fail to enjoy where they are.

1

We sometimes forget that where we are now was once a distant goal. If you look over your life, you might honestly say that your current condition is the result of what used to be your dream. Consider—your marriage, your house, your job, your business, your kids, the list goes on and on—most of these realities were once dreams.

I challenge you not to overlook your progress in the attempt to be progressive; learn to enjoy every moment! Most of us lack the patience to process life's journey properly. We don't recognize incremental success, which is often camouflaged by our pursuit of something bigger or better. We are so eager to reach the next dimension that we do not properly celebrate what God has revealed in our current dimension. This is seen in every spectrum of our lives:

- Intellectually, we're always on a quest for more, without proper celebration of our present progress.
- Financially, we overwork ourselves and never enjoy any rewards.
- Spiritually, we're seeking higher heights and deeper depths, without any balance.

If we are not careful, most of our effort is a result of two diabolical influences—namely, *Comparison* and *Competition.* It's important to confront the spirits of comparison and competition and release the spirit of completion, so that we can enjoy the journey and live our lives with passion. Consider the affect of each spirit for just a moment.

The Spirit of Comparison forces us to evaluate others and their success and progress, not just any ol' body, but those our age, from our background—those with compatible matriculation and experiences. And pastors, we're not left out of the equation. We look at those whose ministries are exploding and whose churches are excelling. Their people seem developed, devoted, and dedicated to their vision, while we are struggling, trying to manage what seems to amount to a daycare filled with adults.

Believe it or not, the Spirit of Comparison is obvious at every level. Those with ten members find themselves comparing their ministry to those with a hundred members; those with a hundred members do the same with those with a thousand, and those with a thousand do the same with those with ten thousand. It never stops. A wealth of pastors, churches, businesses, marriages, and individuals never arrive at their destination or celebrate what God is doing in their lives because they're too busy comparing themselves to others. God gives us all a different grace for the journey assigned us, and I can't enjoy my journey if I'm always spying on others.

> GOD KNOWS EXACTLY WHAT HE'S DOING

The Spirit of Comparison opens the door to the Spirit of Competition, in which you find yourself competing with others, trying to keep up with and be accepted by them. Whatever they're doing becomes your blueprint. Whatever they accomplish becomes your goal. Wherever they live and whatever they drive becomes your dream. Soon, not even God can inspire or influence you, because you're inspired and influenced by others. This is devastating because we, as pastors, influence those unaware of how misguided we are. I challenge you to allow God to complete what he has started in you—the way he designed it and in his time. "Being confident of this very thing, that he

3

which hath begun a good work in you will perform it until the day of Jesus Christ." (Philippians 1:6)

God knows exactly what he's doing, he knows where I'm going, and he knows when I'll arrive, so I might as well enjoy the journey.

- Don't allow others to determine the path you'll take in life; trust the plan of God.
- Visualize your victory.
- Don't change who you are to become someone else.
- Success, growth, and progress are relative!
- Stay focused on your dream, vision, or goal.
- Demand more of yourself.
- Surround yourself with supportive, quality people who respect your destiny.
- Commit yourself to being unstoppable.
- Don't allow your enemies to distract you by competing and comparing.
- Live your life with passion and enjoy every moment!

Principles

- We don't recognize incremental success, which is often camouflaged by our pursuit of something bigger or better.
- It's important to confront the spirits of comparison and competition and release the spirit of completion, so that we can enjoy the journey and live our lives with passion.
- God gives us all a different grace for the journey assigned us.
- God knows exactly what he's doing.

Two

Barren, but Blessed

Take this for the journey:

*When you feel that you have reached the end and you
cannot go one step further, when life seems to be drained of all
purpose—what a wonderful opportunity to start all over again,
to turn over a new page.*
~ Eileen Caddy ~

*It makes us value the inner world;
It trains us to go inside
To the source of peace and inspiration
When we are faced with problems and challenges.*
~ Deepak Chopra ~

God has incredible things in store for us. We cannot deny this truth. We know there is more. It feels like Christmas in October. We know it's not time yet, but we can't contain our excitement. It is the kind of gift that can't be immediately verified. 1 Corinthians 2:9 agrees: "But as it is written, eye hath not seen, nor ear heard, neither have entered into the heart of man, the things which God hath prepared for them that love him."

You may be on the verge of a major turnaround in your life, marriage, or business, but opposing forces can weaken your fortitude. In this chapter, I want to show you how to deal effectively with unseen realities. First, it is essential to interpret properly the problems attached to your victory. Sometimes the closer we get to laying hold of God's promises, the greater the obstacles. When there are delays, break into song. The interim between the process and the promise can make singing almost an impossible task. You say, "I have nothing to sing about," yet I am reminded of Isaiah 54:

Sing, O barren, thou that didst not bear; break forth into singing, and cry aloud, thou that didst not travail with child: for more are the children of the desolate than the children of the married wife, saith the LORD. Enlarge the place of thy tent, and let them stretch forth the curtains of thine habitations: spare not, lengthen thy cords, and strengthen thy stakes; For thou shalt break forth on the right hand and on the left; and thy seed shall inherit the Gentiles, and make the desolate cities to be inhabited. Fear not; for thou shalt not be ashamed: neither be thou confounded; for thou shalt not be put to shame: for thou shalt forget the shame of thy youth, and shalt not remember the reproach of thy widowhood any more. For thy Maker is thine husband; the LORD of hosts is his name; and thy Redeemer the Holy One of Israel; The God of the whole earth shall he be called.

> WHEN THERE ARE DELAYS, BREAK INTO SONG

God wants us to believe before we receive. We must know that we'll get everything God has prepared for us in due season. Enjoy the journey! Let's further explore the expressions of patience and teaching captured in the text. Isaiah encourages us to sing, though we have been barren, unproductive, and unfruitful. This act of will requires courage and confidence in a God who can overcome the troublesome seasons in life. For some, it is difficult to believe in victory when facing unimaginable odds. The Lord wants you to sing in the midst of trials.

The command to "Sing, O barren" speaks volumes. Singing is proof that you are stepping into a new season. Singing with no resolution in sight catapults your faith to a new level. Singing in barren times delivers a fresh release of power to your address. God says that in the absence of increase, great things are about to unfold for you. A major turnaround is moments away. You're about to go from being barren to being blessed!

Someone might ask "how?" While barrenness often seems irreversible, God can open your womb to limitless possibilities. Areas in which you've consistently failed, you are called to excel in. Don't be dismayed. God wants you to expect again! Let's revisit Isaiah 54:2. "Enlarge the place of thy tent...stretch forth the curtains...lengthen thy cords, and strengthen thy stakes." I believe the command is to:

- Enlarge your vision
- Stretch your faith
- Lengthen your expectation
- Strengthen your praise

Enlarge your vision

Sometimes we condense our vision to fit into what we've experienced. Exercise great care because the pressures of life

7

can keep us from seeing beyond where we are. If we are not careful, we will limit ourselves to managing what we have and maintaining our present quality of life. It is imperative to monitor the effects of barrenness, or being barren will overshadow how blessed we can become.

The word "enlarge" means to make bigger, expand, or widen. Your present vision is fine if you plan to remain barren, unproductive, and unfruitful. God has assured us of his plan. It is our responsibility to invite tangible results to manifest in our lives. Do not get mad at God if your current situation does not get better. We must be accountable and willing to enlarge our visions. For some, this means taking a step of faith that defies your current state. As Hebrews 11 declares, faith is the substance of things hoped for and the evidence of things not seen. Enlarging your vision directly correlates to expanding your faith.

Stretch your faith

Your faith must increase. If what you desire does not stretch your faith, you may want to question the source of that desire. God will always pull us out of our comfort zone. God is convinced of his ability to establish and strengthen us. When God has ordained a matter, he will ensure that it comes to pass. Imagine a rubber band stretched as far as it can go. You can actually have a rubber band in your hand, but never see its potential until it's stretched. Similarly, God wants to stretch our faith by pushing us to our limits.

Lengthen your expectations

The word "lengthen" means to pull some more, to extend expectations just a little bit more. Never minimize your expectations; never downsize. You're no longer barren; God has called you to greater, more. Get it into your spirit and shout every time you think about it. God wants to do more for you. More, more, more, more, more! Say it until it's your reality, and extend your expectations to accommodate what God is about to do for you.

Strengthen your praise

Expectation should provoke celebration. My youngest son, Torvon, is proactive and only needs my word to secure his expectation. Even though he does not immediately possess, touch, or see what was promised, he keeps me accountable by reminding me of my verbal commitment to grant his desires. Strengthen your praise! You can't see anything, you don't have it yet, but God's word is good. Praise God when you're without tangible evidence; it's just a matter of time before God blows your mind.

I want you to sing prophetically today. When I started our church, we didn't have enough money to take care of our responsibilities. The enemy preys on us in those seasons. He will cause you to wonder if God really told you to do what you're doing. I found myself second-guessing the promises of God, yet in that season, God gave me a prophetic song that simply said, "It's already done!" I had to sing the song in the midst of the test, but when I did, I felt like I had already won. Praise means, "I agree with God," so strengthen your praise. Let the devil know it's already done. Let him know your bills are already paid, let him know your body is already healed, let him know your family is already saved, let him know the way is already made, and enjoy the journey!

Principles

- It is essential to interpret properly the problems attached to your victory
- When there are delays, break into song.
- Singing is proof that you are stepping into a new season.
- God can open your womb to limitless possibilities.
- God will always pull us out of our comfort zone.
- Expectation should provoke celebration.

THREE

TAKE THE SCENIC ROUTE

Take this for the journey:

Be like a postage stamp. Stick to one thing until you get there.
~Josh Billing~

Great spirits have always encountered violent opposition from
mediocre minds.
The latter cannot understand it when a man does not thought-
lessly submit to hereditary prejudices but honestly and
courageously uses his intelligence.
~Albert Einstein ~

Go confidently in the direction of your dreams. Live the life
you've imagined!
~ Author Unknown ~

One of the most life-enhancing abilities we can develop is the ability to enjoy the journey. We want so much to be living the reality we seek that we sometimes forget that life *is* the journey and the journey *is* life. Enjoy every moment of your journey between here and there; anticipate the next great adventure. As Abraham-Hicks teaches, "If you're not feeling good, if you're not having fun, if you're not enjoying the journey, you're really missing the point of being here."

The challenge before us is to look at those things we wouldn't normally see—the things that most times go unnoticed and unappreciated. Take the scenic route. Notice all that's good and wholesome that has somehow faded in the hustle and bustle. We have become so outcome-oriented that we fail to see how we would benefit if we just relaxed and took pleasure in where we are and what we are doing. How much of today are you really enjoying?

COUNT THE
TRAILERS
IN YOUR
LIFE

Today is so filled with responsibilities, between preparing for work or school, taking the kids to school, fixing lunch, ironing clothes, cleaning, cooking, pumping gas, actually working, getting off early and rushing back for the kids, taking them to practice, that it's easy to convince yourself that today is not to be enjoyed.

I've known people who worked their entire lives, died, and never really enjoyed the journey, not even a day, because they were so focused on what they wanted to accomplish it took the joy out of it. Now, don't get me wrong:

- We should be goal oriented
- We should have dreams
- We should be focused

But life is to be enjoyed!

As long as we live, we will aspire towards something greater than what we presently have. God engineered us this way. Yet it is important to celebrate our accomplishments. If I fail to acknowledge my progress, I may open the door to failure and frustration. Even if we are not where we desire to be in life, we must celebrate that God has brought us a very long way. Have you really noticed how successful you have become?

- Have you considered that you have been married now for fourteen years?
- Have you acknowledged the progress your children are making in school or sports?
- Or that your business is about to celebrate its first anniversary?
- How about applauding yourself for making it a full day on your diet?
- Did you pause to celebrate the fact that you successfully quit smoking or drinking?

It is important to commend yourself for taking small steps towards your goals. Start by doing the below activities consistently:

- Celebrate yourself
- Take time out for yourself
- Recognize your own value
- Appreciate yourself

Most individuals only start to understand and appreciate life during their later years. I am blessed to share a unique and precious relationship with Mother Williams, a long-time member of my father's church. I love listening to Mother Williams whenever I stop by to see her. She thanks God for everything: life, health, strength, food, clothes, water, legs, eyes—the list goes on. I respect her approach to life. Mother Williams, now in her late eighties, expresses gratitude for things that often are taken for granted. She demonstrates a wonderful enjoyment of life's journey. I learned valuable lessons from her. First, life is a process that involves change.

- New seasons
- New dimensions
- New experiences

...are always on the horizon. It is great to have a plan for the future, but it should not stop me from enjoying all that my current season brings. Below are tips to help you enjoy today:

- This is my day, the best day of my entire life!
- I have the power to handle whatever comes my way today!
- I will move competently through my tasks today, embracing the spirit of accomplishment!
- I know what I want in life (today), and I will do whatever it takes to get it!

Take time to appreciate and celebrate your life and all that God has blessed you with. The next time your kids invite you to admire something they made, take time to celebrate their accomplishment. This is called taking the scenic route. It requires us to consciously pay attention to things you might normally overlook. The next time your spouse asks your opinion about their physical appearance, compliment and affirm his or her beauty.

Learn to enjoy every aspect of your life, marriage, family, and business—you will live longer. Take a moment to reflect. Admit how good God has been to you. Enjoy the simple things in life. Get joy out of the small things. I recall as a child counting individual trailers as we waited for long trains to end. The wait did not seem as long because we were too busy enjoying counting.

Is it possible that you have been ignoring how successful you already have become? Stop! Put everything on hold, count the trailers in your life, and have fun doing it. Enjoy it. Gather your family together, grab a bowl of popcorn, get out the photo albums, and have a ball.

Laugh
Cry
Get mad
Get even
Tell jokes
But whatever you do, *enjoy it!*

Remember, this is the day which the Lord hath made; we will rejoice and be glad in it.

Principles
- How much of today are you really enjoying?
- As long as we live, we will aspire towards something greater than what we presently have.

15

- If I fail to acknowledge my progress, I may open the door to failure and frustration.
- It is important to commend yourself for making small steps towards finishing your goals.
- We are not wired to stay in the same place or on the same level.
- Count the trailers in your life.

FOUR

IT'S WORKING TOGETHER!

Take this for the journey:

Here is the Divine Dichotomy...The way to get there is to be there. Just be where you choose to get! It's that simple.
~ Neale Donald Walsch, from Conversations with God, Book 3 *~*

All successful people, men and women, are big dreamers. They imagine what their future could be, ideal in every respect, and then they work every day toward their distant vision, that goal or purpose.
~ Brian Tracy ~

Actually, we have no problems—we have opportunities for which we should give thanks. An error we refuse to correct has many lives. It takes courage to face one's own shortcomings, and wisdom to do something about them.
~ Edgar Cayce ~

And we know that all things work together for good to those who love God.
~ Romans 8:28 ~

Pursuing your goals is much like putting a puzzle together. You have to work at it piece by piece, and since you will spend most of your time trying to make and see progress, you must enjoy what you're doing in order to finish. Take joy from the process, and use the small successes to fuel your continued efforts. My mom has a special grace to start and finish jigsaw puzzles. She amazes me. Seeing all the pieces of the puzzle come together is incredible. But the actual puzzle has already been figured out, broken into pieces, and put into a box, just so my mom can put it together again. The key is not just to have all of the pieces in your possession, but also to keep the outcome before you. Do not throw away the box! The box provides the explanation. Keeping the vision before you is one of the keys to obtaining your desired outcome in life, business, marriage, or ministry.

DON'T THROW AWAY THE BOX!

I was invited to speak in an unfamiliar city in Florida. I asked my staff to provide me with detailed directions explaining the complicated journey. An invitation was not enough. I needed help connecting all the roads, highways, streets, and boulevards. They were all headed somewhere, but perhaps not where I needed to be. Directions were given: head north on I-95. Often we referred to the directions, checking to make sure we were headed in the right direction. It sounds like that jigsaw puzzle— the box is as important as all the little pieces on the coffee table. It is a revelation of the outcome, and it serves as a road map, making sure that every turn agrees with your destination. Now, if the box is needed to ensure the jigsaw puzzle's outcome, and directions are needed to secure my arrival in Florida, why approach life's journey without a goal on which to focus?

If you never define your bull's eye, you can simply throw an arrow in any direction, and wherever it lands, you can mark that spot. By those standards, you always win, goal setting is never necessary, and focus is a waste of time. When this is the case, everything you set out to do is subject to change, and so we go through life without accomplishing anything. It's important to define your goals, because in doing so you invite discipline into your life, which is needed to bring all the pieces together.

Have you ever met a person with big dreams? I mean big, big dreams—but they were not disciplined enough to take the actions necessary to manifest them? Taking action not only allows you to realize the outcome, but it commits you to the process. You must commit to the process to produce the outcome, and since the most of your time will be spent manifesting destiny, or producing the outcome, should you not find joy in the journey?

- Define your goals
- Take action
- Commit to the process

The enemy will try to convince you that something is missing. He will say you do not have enough education, or you're not the right color, or everyone else is better than you are—and all of what he says may be true, but you have what it takes to produce the outcome that is in your heart. You have all the pieces to your puzzle; now rebuke the spirit that causes you to second-guess the grace on your life.

When I put together a puzzle, I start with the corners and then move on to the edges, because they provide definition. Definition will steady your focus, so take your time, and be clear about where you're going. Starting over is difficult even when it's in God's will. How much more so do you think it is when we were not clear about where we were going? Finally, be persistent. Do not allow challenges to keep you from the outcome in your spirit; most of your challenges will help you organize your life to receive God's best. Your goal should be a present part of your life, offering you direction and encouragement. Enjoy the journey!

"It is not because things are difficult that we do not dare, it is because we do not dare that they are difficult."
~ Lucius Annaeus Seneca ~

Hold fast to dreams, for without them we are like birds with broken wings.
~ Chinese Proverb ~

Principles
- Do not throw away the box!
- You must commit to the process to produce the outcome.
- Rebuke the spirit that causes you to second-guess the grace on your life.

FIVE

GOD HAS NOT CHANGED HIS MIND

Take this for the journey:

Your vision will become clear only when you look into your heart ...Who looks outside, dreams. Who looks inside, awakens.
~ Carl Jung

Love is what we were born with. Fear is what we learned here.
The spiritual journey is the relinquishment - or unlearning - of
fear and the acceptance of love back into our hearts.
~ Marianne Williamson from A Return to Love *~*

If you don't know where you are going, then how will you get there? Visualize! Make pictures in your mind. See the destination. Imagine your arrival. Dream in perfect detail. See yourself the way you want to be when you arrive. See yourself arriving. Make yourself a road map and study it every day until you know the way and the destination by heart.
~ Bryce Courtenay ~

So much that I expect hinges upon God keeping his word, and every now and then, I am challenged in my expectation. Some say, "If he were going to do anything, he would have done it by now." It's hard to believe that he is going to do something when it's not done yet.

God has not changed his mind. Your status may change, your financial stability may change, your friendships may change, but God has not changed his mind. I cannot allow what is changing to change my definition of God. He is still God that speaks and brings it to pass. Check out what he says to Abram:

"Now the Lord had said unto Abram, get thee out of thy country, and from thy kindred, and from thy father's house, unto a land that I will shew thee." (Genesis 12:1)

God challenged him to go beyond the familiar places and familiar people, into an unknown place. When God is organizing destiny, he moves you from around that which is comfortable because he has so much more in store for you. He was putting Abram in a position to be blessed beyond what he had ever been. When things are changing, it does not mean that God has changed his mind—he is just positioning me to possess more! Consider Genesis 12:1-3:

Now the Lord had said unto Abram, Get thee out of thy country, and from thy kindred, and from thy father's house, unto a land that I will shew thee: And I will make of thee a great nation, and I will bless thee, and make thy name great; and thou shalt be a blessing: I will bless them that bless thee, and curse him that curseth thee: and in thee shall all families of the earth be blessed.

God spoke, and Abram's life changed. Abram obeyed, it says in verse 4: "So Abram departed." But this is what throws us off—God said it, we obeyed, so why hasn't anything happened yet? We conclude that perhaps God has changed his mind. Check out Abram in Genesis 15:8: "And he said, Lord God, whereby shall I know that I shall inherit it?"

Abram was not experiencing what God had promised, so he asked, "How do I know what you have promised will come to pass? It's been some time, and nothing is happening."

So we begin to downsize our vision and dreams, but hold on. God has not changed his mind. He had to remind Abram. "And he said unto him, I am the Lord that brought thee out of Ur of the Chaldees, to give thee this land to inherit it."

Yes! I challenged you to leave familiar territory and go away from familiar people. Yes! I said I was going to make you a great nation and bless you, and make your name great and bless them that bless you and curse them that curse you, and yes! I said in thee shall all the families of the earth be blessed. Yes! You obeyed my voice, and no, you have not seen anything yet, but let me tell you this, Abram—I have not changed my mind!

> YOU MUST STAND ON THE PROMISES OF GOD

God has not changed his mind about your destiny, healing, deliverance, increase, promotion, or family. You must stand on the promises of God. Check out Abram's testimony:

As it is written, I have made thee a father of many nations, before him, whom he believed, *even* God, who quickened the dead, and calleth those things which be not as though they were. Who against hope believed in hope, that he might become the father of many nations, according to that which was spoken, so shall thy seed be. And being not weak in faith, he considered not his own body now dead, when he was about an hundred years old, neither yet the deadness of Sara's womb: He staggered not at the promise of God through unbelief; but was strong in faith, giving glory to God; And being fully persuaded that, what he had promised, he was able also to perform.

When Abram started believing, it was done! The process produced the promise. Your process cannot negate the fact that God has not changed his mind.

Principles

- God has not changed his mind—he is just positioning me to possess more!
- You must stand on the promises of God.
- Your process cannot negate the fact that God has not changed his mind.

Six

Undetected Victories

Take this for the journey:

It is good to have an end to journey towards,
but it is the journey that matters in the end.
~ Ursula K. LeGuin, novelist ~

People who say it cannot be done should not
interrupt those who are doing it.
~ Author Unknown ~

"Come to the edge," he said. They said, "We are afraid." "Come to
the edge," he said. They came. He pushed them...and they flew.
~ Guillauame Apollinaire ~

We believe that victories must be something major, but really, even the small things are worth celebrating. We all tend to undervalue our small successes. We fail to realize that the evolution of destiny is experienced daily. Victories often are concealed on the path to our destinies. They go undetected because they are underrated.

We must re-evaluate our understanding of victory and our progress towards self-fulfillment and purposeful living. Every day lived presents a unique opportunity to develop in a different area. Ask yourself, "How have I developed today?" Perhaps you read a book that increased your intellectual prowess or had an experience that added to your wisdom. The potential to improve is always present.

There are many reasons to daily assess our development. Often, our tendency to reserve our energy for what Fred Sanford coined "the big one" obscures our view of the resources available to us. Invaluable insight can be attained when we allow lessons to serve as a platform for growth. "Positive reinforcement" as a predictor of continued success comes to mind. We gain momentum when we make progress. I am reminded of a baby's transition from crawling to walking. We applaud the baby for each effort to stand

> WE MUST RE-EVALUATE OUR UNDERSTANDING OF VICTORY

erect, firmly hold onto a parent's hand, and take small steps. This example vividly symbolizes the path to progress. It is not an overnight wonder, but a daily trek. Positive steps encourage us to continue the journey, but the potential for the opposite effect is also present. Unnoticed victories can lead to frustration and failure. Simply put, our inability to embrace the blessing of daily progress can make failure inevitable. Galatians 6:9 reads, "And let us not be weary in well doing: for in due season we shall reap, if we faint not."

Consider the person who becomes weary in well doing. This passage warns against fainting. Fainting may be the result of frustration or not being able to detect victory or progress in its purest form. It is so important to highlight simple successes and victories. Doing so enables us to guard against weariness and failure. The notion of reaping in due season has captivated us; many times, we discount and downplay the small steps. We forget to celebrate them with the same intensity and vigor. Your ministry may not be huge, but it still can and should be celebrated for the successes achieved on its own merit.

Leaders of smaller ministries with the capacity to grow and develop must not deprive themselves of their victories. When my wife and I first got married, we hung out with other married couples. Most were more established and had more money than we did, but we had peace. When we moved into our first apartment, we were unable to furnish it as the other couples did. We made the best of what we had. We visited the Goodwill and purchased a nice sofa, a huge whatnot stand, a couple of lamps, and a nice bed. We were grateful for and proud of our little apartment and invited the other couples over. In hindsight, I am sure they probably made fun of us. We didn't care. We were too busy celebrating our small victory! You may be in a similar situation. Celebrate your victory. Can we pray?

Thank you, Lord Jesus, for insight into that which we have underestimated. Thank you, because through this chapter, we have developed appreciation for what you have blessed us with and enabled us to do. Thine shall the glory be forever, Amen!

Principles
- We must re-evaluate our understanding of victory.
- Invaluable insight can be attained when we allow lessons to serve as a platform for growth.
- Unnoticed victories can lead to frustration and failure.

- The notion of reaping in due season has captivated us; many times, we discount and downplay the small steps.

SEVEN

TRAVEL LIGHT

Take this for the journey:

*Keep away from people who try to belittle your ambitions.
Small people always do that, but the really great make you feel
that you too can become great.*
~ Mark Twain ~

*People are always blaming their circumstances for what they
are. I don't believe in circumstances. The people who get on in
this world are the people who get up and look for the circumstances they want. And if they can't, make them.*
~ George Bernard Shaw ~

*Say what you mean and act how you feel, because those who
matter don't mind, and those who mind don't matter.*
~ Dr. Seuss ~

He that cannot endure the bad will not live to see the good.
~ Anonymous ~

*Wherefore seeing we also are compassed about with so great a
cloud of witnesses, let us lay aside every weight, and the sin
which doth so easily beset us, and let us run with patience the
race that is set before us, Looking unto Jesus the author and
finisher of our faith; who for the joy that was set before him endured the cross, despising the shame, and is set down at the
right hand of the throne of God.*
~ Hebrews 12:1-2 ~

A valuable part of enjoying the journey depends on our
ability to possess the spirit of release. Consider this
the B clause of verse 1. "Let us lay aside every
weight, and the sin which doth so easily beset us, and let us run
with patience the race that is set before us."

The text challenges us to finish the journey. God tells us to
"lay aside every weight." Now, "weight" here is a burden, load,
power, or influence that hinders your progress. I like this because if we are honest, we will agree that some weights in our
lives really hinder our progress.

When I was a young traveling evangelist, I would preach
five nights of revival. It was awesome to minister in different
cities and meet new people. I wanted to look good, so when
packing for these revivals, I packed five different pairs of shoes,
five different suits, five different shirts and ties, my daywear,
and my after-church wear, which all required a different pair of
shoes, and so to do a five-night revival, I traveled with five or
six big bags. A dear friend of mine came to hang out with me
for one of my revivals. He only had one suit bag and one duffle
bag, and when he saw what I brought, he said, "Torrey, you

would be better off if you learned to travel light. You have too much stuff! Take a blue suit and a black suit, a few white shirts, a pair of black shoes, and switch up your ties? Then you would be down to one suit bag and one duffle bag."

I don't travel with all those bags anymore; I learned to travel light. Have you ever wondered why you are so exhausted and not excited? Could it be that you're traveling with too much stuff yourself? Some of our weight or load is the wrong people. For much of our lives, we carry other folk. We carry them financially when we allow them to live off the fruit of our labor. We carry them spiritually when we allow them to drain us without trying to develop themselves. We carry them emotionally when we hold on to them, even though they have moved on—when we mourn and lament over what used to be. All of those bags, weights, influences, and powers hinder our mobility. We would get farther and have more if we did not carry so much weight. We could probably be closer to God. If you're going to enjoy the journey, you have to lay aside the weight. Not just the convenient weights or the weights that are visible—every weight.

> YOU HAVE TOO MUCH STUFF!

Think about traveling in a car. If I am to have a successful journey, I must take stuff out of the trunk so I can travel with what I really need. Some of us really do have too much junk in our trunk. We are loaded down with things that hinder our progress and crowd out what we really need. Decide what you really need in order:

- To be successful
- To have joy

- To have peace
- To accomplish your goals

You may discover that you have been carrying too much. Travel light, don't over-burden yourself, lay aside every weight, and enjoy the journey! Can we pray?

God, we thank you for wisdom in this matter, we acknowledge your plan to take us to a new place in life, and God, we release every weight that stops our progress and release ourselves into your custody now, in Jesus' name, Amen.

Principles

- If we are honest, we will agree that some weights in our lives really hinder our progress.
- You have too much stuff!

EIGHT

RESPECT THE PROCESS

Take this for the journey:

A life without dreams is like a garden without flowers.
~ Author Unknown ~

Often people attempt to live their lives backwards. They try to have more things, or more money, in order to do more of what they want so they will be happier. The way it actually works is the reverse. You must first be who you really are, then do what you need to do, in order to have what you want.
~ Margaret Young ~

You have to leave the city of your comfort and go into the wilderness of your intuition. What you'll discover will be wonderful. What you'll discover is yourself.
~ Alan Alda ~

There are no secrets to success. It is the result of preparation, hard work, and learning from failures.
~ Colin Powell ~

A journey of a thousand miles must begin with a single step.
~ Lao-Tzu ~

You must have long-range goals to keep you from being frus-
trated by short-range failures.
~ Charles C. Noble ~

"And let us run with patience the race that is set before us." (Hebrews 12:1) Everything in life is a process. Aspects are always developing, advancing, and progressing. As long as we exist, we will always be headed somewhere, reaching higher, or attempting new feats. Running without patience is why most people never get to the finishing line. Running with patience challenges us to respect the process.

In this usage, the word "patience" means to endure and persist. When we think of a race, one of the first things that come to mind is the finish line; however, before we can get to the finish line, we must endure the process. If we fail to respect it, the race is no longer relevant. If you have ever participated in a race, you know that you don't need endurance before you start, nor do you need persistence after you've crossed the finish line, but you need both while you're in the race because the race is design to demand the best that you have. So consider before, during, and after:

Before

Before is a time of planning or preparation. In this phase, there are few challenges because it's all theory; nothing is solid. Things are subject to change. Most people don't stick to the discipline of the journey because they had no discipline in their

34

planning. The Bible says, "A double minded man is unstable in all his ways." (James 1:8) Instability is the expectation of a double-minded man. It's important that in our season of planning and preparation we develop a surety about our destination, so that when challenges come, we will stick to our plan.

> EVERYTHING IN LIFE IS A PROCESS

Many people do not enjoy their journey because they never developed convictions. They planned according to what they saw others doing, and they equate process with failure because they don't understand that it is a part of the journey. They become frustrated. In our time of planning and preparation, we must know that it's the will of God for us to start.

During

Now consider "during." This is the journey. This is what is to be enjoyed, not because everything is going according to schedule or because there's no conflict, but because it's the will of God. This is where the enemy tries to confuse us. He wants you to live a life of uncertainty because if we ever discover the will of God, it will not matter how it looks, feels, or is. You'll know that because it's his will, everything is going to be all right. Romans 8:28 must become a reality: "And we know that all things work together for good to them that love God, to them who are the called according to *His* purpose."

Nobody or nothing can change this fact, and when you have this assurance on the journey, you are a dangerous person. You cannot be stopped, blocked, or hindered.

After

My "after" is proof that God keeps his word. I mean, who but God can give you a vision, organize your opposition, and then bring you to your expectation in one piece? Dr. Anthony Wilcots would say, "He is a mighty God." By the time it's over and we're out, we will have a mandate to praise him, so my "after" is an opportunity to praise the God of my salvation.

Every journey has a before, a during, and an after, and we must respect the process. We cannot omit any phase, because by doing so, we disrespect the order of God. He gives you a Word, and then he tries the Word that he has given you. Then he manifests the Word for his glory. "He's a mighty God."

<u>Principles</u>

- Everything in life is a process.
- As long as we exist, we will always be headed somewhere.
- Most people don't stick to the discipline of the journey because they had no discipline in their planning.
- You cannot be stopped, blocked, or hindered.
- My "after" is an opportunity to praise the God of my salvation.
- He's a mighty God.

Nine

Are You Ready Yet?

Take this for the journey:

We learn wisdom from failure much more than from success. We often discover what will do by finding out what will not do. And probably he who never made a mistake never made a discovery.
~ Samuel Smiles ~

Trials are but lessons that you failed to learn, presented once again. So, where you made a faulty choice before, you can now make a better one, and thus escape all pain that what you chose before has brought to you.
~ A Course in Miracles ~

Adversity has the effect of eliciting talents which, in prosperous circumstances, would have lain dormant.
~ Horace ~

God challenges us to enjoy the journey to our destiny. In this chapter, we will explore the importance of balancing our approaches to trials and triumphs. The time between fulfillment of the promise and the process is a monumental factor when we consider God's plan. We underestimate the time it took for Abraham to become the father of many nations or for Job to receive his double portion, or David to become king. We focus more on the *product* of God's word and not the *process*.

Sometimes our desire to end trials quickly and get out unscathed obscures the plan of God. However, God's purpose is developed in and through us while on the journey. Let's examine God's method of exposing his wisdom to the children of Israel in Deuteronomy: 8:2-3:

And thou shalt remember all the way which the LORD thy God led thee these forty years in the wilderness, to humble thee, and to prove thee, to know what was in thine heart, whether thou wouldest keep his commandments, or not. And he humbled thee, and suffered thee to hunger, and fed thee with manna, which thou knewest not, neither did thy fathers know; that he might make thee know that man doth not live by bread only, but by every *word* that proceedeth out of the mouth of the LORD doth man live.

Like the children of Israel, God often reminds us to esteem his word above challenging circumstances. Trials serve as a training ground for victorious living. God permits situations to humble us. God never intended the children of Israel to die in the wilderness after they eluded Pharaoh's army and exited Egypt. Their safe arrival in their place of promise was always at the forefront of his mind. However, their behavior disconnected them. The children of Israel did not value God's wisdom and provisions. Nor did they appreciate the fact that God delivered them from the hand of the enemy. God did not leave them helpless. He humbled them.

How many people do you know who have died while on their way to fulfilling their dreams, unwrapping their vision, or manifesting their destiny? How many times has God intervened in our affairs to reiterate that his plan for our lives must match his timing and purpose?

Humility is a powerful weapon in God's arsenal. The word "humble" means to feel less proud or convinced of one's own importance. Humility and death of self-will, in exchange for submission to God's divine plan, prepares us to glorify God in all our endeavors.

God exposed me to humbling seasons to prepare me for promotion. There were times God let all of the air out of my balloon and I found myself humbled beyond expression. My relationship with God soared to new dimensions when I recognized how privileged I was to have him in my life as a coach, comforter, and supreme instructor.

I learned to serve God and his people because I love him. I lost the spirit of entitlement when I realized that God did not owe me anything. I was thankful to be alive. I gained a sense of appreciation and value.

- Declaration without manifestation is humbling
- Self perception without proof is humbling
- Being anointed without opportunity is humbling
- Being gifted without an open door is humbling
- Having vision without provision is humbling

Like the children of Israel, God humbles and proves us. In Deuteronomy 8:2, prove actually means, "to test." God will test us before he promotes us. Tests determine if we are ready to receive and maintain the blessings that we think we want.

God tested the children of Israel in the wilderness. His test revealed that they were out of Egypt, but the bondage of Egypt was not out of them. Egypt represented the old mindset, thought processes, and behaviors. Even though they physically left Egypt, they were not ready to embrace Canaan, their place of promise. God is not wasteful. He will not release a promise to those who can't handle it. He makes provisions for us to grow in grace and submit to his guidance. However, if we are still governed by our old nature, we are not ready for his promises.

> TRAILS SERVE AS A TRAINING GROUND FOR VICTORIOUS LIVING

I have a teenage son—Torrey Jr. Last year, I attended a conference with one of his teachers. She acknowledged that Torrey failed her class because he wasted the opportunity to learn. Instead of completing his assignments, he chose to play around and disturb others. He opted not to apply himself, even though he possessed the intellectual ability to do so. How many of us resemble Torrey? When we fail our tests, do we spend too much time focusing on matters irrelevant to God's plan? God will test us until we prove that we are ready for the next dimension. His tests determine if we are ready to receive and maintain the blessings that we think we want.

He exposes:

- The quality of our commitment to God

- The level of our commitment to his plan and our ultimate destiny
- Our motive (motivation)
- Our obedience
- The degree of our fortitude to endure under pressure
- Our ability to manage conflict
- The strength of our Word and prayer life

I believe the place that God desires to take us is not conditional, but revelational. When I possess a revelation of God's investment into my life, I'll willingly discipline my motives, walk in total obedience, increase my devotion and prayer time, advance in the Word, and give God the glory that he deserves. Until this is your testimony, you will hinder God's best for your life.

Principles

- We focus more on the *product* of God's word and not the *process*.
- Trials serve as a training ground for victorious living.
- Humility is a powerful weapon in God's arsenal.
- Humility and death of self-will, in exchange for submission to God's divine plan, prepares us to glorify God in all our endeavors.
- His tests determine if we are ready to receive and maintain the blessings that we think we want.

TEN

FROM START TO FINISH

Take this for the journey:

Things are always at their best in the beginning.
~ Pascal ~

The beginning is the most important part of the work.
~ Plato ~

And in the end, it's not the years in your life that count, it's the
life in your years.
~ Abraham Lincoln ~

Difficulties are opportunities to better things; they are stepping-
stones to greater experience. Perhaps some day you will be
thankful for some temporary failure in a particular direction.
When one door closes, another always opens, as a natural law
it has to be, to balance.
~ Brian Adams ~

Pain by itself is merely pain, but the experience of pain coupled
with an understanding that the pain serves a worthy purpose is
suffering. Suffering can be endured because there is a reason

43

for it that is worth the effort. What is more worthy of your pain than the evolution of your soul?
~ Gary Zukav ~

Although I was born January 3, 1974, I existed in the mind of God, waiting on my time of manifestation, long before. God tells Jeremiah, "Before I formed thee in the belly I knew thee; and before thou camest forth out of the womb I sanctified thee, and I ordained thee a prophet unto the nations." This means that although the plan of God is experienced from start to finish, it was finished before it started.

Consider Isaiah 46:9-10:

R emember the former things of old: for I am God, and there is none else; I am God, and there in none like me. Declaring the end from the beginning, and from ancient times the things that are not yet done, saying, My counsel shall stand, and I will do all my pleasure.

This should make you shout, because what you are about to start is finished! God is so awesome that he factors in good and bad, ups and downs, and still declares your victory. So stay focused. Allow nothing to deter you from your destiny.

Wherefore seeing we also are compassed about with so great a cloud of witnesses, let us lay aside every weight, and the sin which doth so easily beset us, and let us run with patience the race that is set before us, Looking unto Jesus the author and finisher of our faith; who for the joy tat was set before him endured the cross, despising the shame, and is set down at the right hand of the throne of God. (Hebrews 12:1)

Although the writer of Hebrew takes an end-time perspective, it is applicable to the many destinies on our way to our eternal destiny. Every test transports us to another level.

Remember high school finals? I had mixed emotions. I was nervous, but anticipated the test that would send me to the next level. A year or so later, there would be another major test, and again I would have mixed emotions, only to pass the test and move on to the next level. Tests in school are no different from the tests of life; we are constantly introduced to trials that take us to new levels in God, so expect the tests, anticipate the next level, but don't forget to enjoy the journey.

Expect the tests!

James 1:2 reminds us "My brethren, count it all joy when ye fall into diverse temptations; Know *this*, that the trying of your faith worketh patience."

The apostle James encourages us to have joyful expectations in every situation. He argues that the testing of your faith produces endurance. Why do I need endurance if there is nothing to come? The test reminds us that something greater is just up the road. If you expect anything from God, expect a test to qualify you for the promotion. Your tests are road signs that let you know you're almost there. Hallelujah!

James 1:12 declares, "Blessed is the man that endureth temptation: for when he is tried, he shall receive the crown of life, which the Lord hath promised to them that love Him."

Again, the apostle James takes another end-time perspective, and says the endurance of a test releases the promises of

God. Just think, you were going to give up and throw in the towel, but the devil is a liar. Remind every foe, every enemy, and every adversary that you expected it. You have great things in store for you; you have only to go through this test.

The Bible is filled with those who have had tests that were

> A DELAY DOES
> NOT DETERMINE
> YOUR DESTINY

only precursors to great victories! Joseph was tested before his promotion, so was David, Abraham, and Jesus. In Romans 8:18, the apostle Paul says, "For I reckon that the sufferings of this present time *are* not worthy *to be compared* with the glory which shall be revealed in us."

What you're going through is only setting you up for greater!

Anticipate the Next Level

"Let us hold fast the profession of our faith without wavering; for He *is* faithful that promised...Cast not away therefore your confidence, which hath great recompense of reward. For ye have need of patience, that, after ye have done the will of God, ye might receive the promise." (Hebrews 10:23, 35-36)

One of our greatest weapons is the "spirit of anticipation." We can never be restricted to a mindset of defeat if we anticipate something greater. Sometimes efforts are challenged by delays. I have been in the airport, on my way somewhere, but met with complications despite having a boarding pass in my hand and luggage on my shoulder. I could not go anywhere, but I refused to go home. I knew that once the complications and delays were over, once this season was over, I was getting on the plane. A delay does not determine your destiny. Hold fast to the profession of your faith. Don't cast away your confidence. Anticipate the next level of victory, peace, joy, and blessing.

When you expect the tests that are designed to usher you into fulfillment, and continue to anticipate the next level, you can't help but get ready for manifestation, increase, and an outstanding outcome. It's already done!

Principles

- This means that although the plan of God is experienced from start to finish, it was finished before it started.
- Every test transports us to another level.
- The test reminds us that something greater is just up the road.
- Your tests are road signs that let you know you're almost there.
- The endurance of a test releases the promises of God. What you're going through is only setting you up for greater!
- A delay does not determine your destiny.

ELEVEN

LORD, SHOW ME YOUR PLAN

Take this for the journey:

You take your life in your own hands, and what happens?
A terrible thing: no one to blame.
~ Erica Jong ~

Unless you start doing something different,
you are in for more of the same.
~ Author Unknown ~

The truth is that our finest moments are most likely to occur
when we are feeling deeply uncomfortable, unhappy, or unful-
filled. For it is only in such moments, propelled by our
discomfort, that we are likely to step out of our ruts and start
searching for different ways or truer answers.
~ M. Scott Peck ~

A good plan is like a road map: It shows the final destination
and usually the best way to get there.
~ H. Stanley Judd ~

For I know the thoughts [PLAN] that I think toward you,
[HAVE FOR YOU] saith the LORD, thoughts of peace, and not
of evil, to give you an expected end.
~ Jeremiah 29:11 ~

The word plan is defined as "an arrangement, scheme, outline, or sketch." Life is filled with plans, blueprints, ingredients, and roadmaps. When used correctly, these tools usually result in success. To experience success in life, marriage, ministry, business, or investments, a plan is necessary. Not just any plan—the plan must agree with God's intended outcome for our lives.

I recently learned, firsthand, the benefits of having a plan. Cooking has never been my favorite pastime. Yet, while waiting for dinner one Sunday afternoon, I began to experiment in the kitchen. I saw the ingredients of banana pudding listed on the side of the Nabisco vanilla wafers box. I could produce a delicious banana pudding if I followed the recipe. I had an idea of the process involved in making banana pudding. My mother and others had often made it. I assumed it was simply a matter of mixing cookies, pudding, and bananas. How hard could it be?

However, as I read the recipe, I was forced to change my preconceptions. The actual process differed significantly from what I imagined. I had to stick to the plan on the box if I wanted to prepare the banana pudding as described. I followed the instructions and was blessed to watch my family and friends devour the dessert.

I often wonder what would have become of the banana pudding had I disregarded the recipe. Much like Nabisco, God has a plan for our destiny. "There are many plans in a man's heart, Nevertheless it's the Lord's counsel that will stand." (NKJ, Proverbs 19:21)

I now realize that the more I follow the plan, the more I produce the expected outcome. No one consistently wanders upon success in any area. There must be a plan instituted by God. Jeremiah 29:11 agrees. "For I know the thoughts [PLANS] that I have toward you, saith the LORD, thoughts [PLANS] of peace, and not of evil to give you an expected end."

True submission to the plan helps secure our destiny. Failure to follow plans can have catastrophic results, particularly in times of uncertainty and change. Plans are like a leaf in the wind; circumstances can alter them. Consider how leaves shift on windy days or how rain interferes with travel. During challenging seasons, God encourages us to revisit the plan and make adjustments to secure completion. Like Abram in Genesis 18, we must remain diligent and cautious during trials. Anxious, uncalculated movements can leave us unfulfilled.

There are times when life demands a shift. Be sensitive to God's timing; don't refuse to move because things don't seem to be going the way you planned. If you want to enjoy the journey, you must seek God and to allow him to show you his plan! Several translations of Isaiah 14:24 provide insight into why following God's plan is so important:

- The LORD of hosts has sworn: As I have resolved, so shall it be; as I have proposed, so shall it stand. KJV

- The LORD of hosts has sworn: As I have resolved, so shall it be; as I have proposed, so shall it stand. NABWRNT
- The LORD All-Powerful has made this promise: These things will happen exactly as I planned them: they will happen exactly as I set them up. NCV
- The LORD of hosts has sworn, saying, Surely, as I have thought, so it shall come to pass, and as I have purposed, so it shall stand. NKJV

The passage clearly affirms the sovereignty of God. It suggests that God does not wonder where he's taking us or where we'll end up. He knows our destination. If I am to enjoy the journey, I cannot waste time meandering aimlessly. God's plan gives direction, meaning, and purpose to our endeavors. Success in ministry, marriage, business, and school starts by acknowledging that God's plan is the equivalent of success!

This actually means that God's plan is necessary for those who seek success. Proverbs 3:5-6 reminds us to "Trust the LORD with all thine heart; and lean not unto thine own understanding. In all thy ways acknowledge him, and he shall direct thy paths." When God reveals his plan, don't be surprised if some of your present connections become less stable.

Many times, we miss our moment because we are unwilling to embrace God's plan when and if it confronts our dependence on relationships that we think are essential to our destiny. Sometimes yielding and surrendering to God's plan requires us to disconnect from our comfort zones. Consider what God told Abram in Genesis 12:1. "Now the LORD has said unto Abram,

Get thee out of thy country, and from thy kindred, and from thy father's house, unto a land that I will shew thee."

Disconnection from familiar places, people, and things is usually one of the first demands God makes when he's exposing his plan for our lives. To experience the plan of God, Abram detached himself from his family and home state. He had to trust God while following an unpredictable path to his destiny as "the Father of many nations." This is a key aspect in enjoying the journey—confidence that even if God commands us to leave familiar surroundings, he never leaves us without resources. He told Abram: "I will make of thee a great nation, and I will bless thee, and make thy name great; and thou shalt be a blessing: And I will bless them that bless thee, and curse him that curseth thee: and in thee shall all families of the earth be blessed."

> GOD HAS A PLAN FOR OUR DESTINY

God secured Abram's success with his plan. We can glean insight about enjoying the journey from this passage. Our provisions in life are connected to the plan of God. Learning to wait on God's scheduled harvest is a facet of enjoying the journey. The choice is ours. We can choose to fulfill God's plan for our lives by walking in fertility and fruitfulness, or we can allow mediocrity to limit us. "Behold, I set before you this day a blessing and a curse; A blessing, if ye obey the commandments of the LORD your God, which I command you this day." (Deuteronomy 11:26-27)

Choose God's plan and enjoy the journey. This starts with. "Lord, show me your plan…"

- For my life
- For my marriage

53

- For my career
- For my business
- For raising my children
- For my finances
- For my health
- For my relationship(s)

Lord, show me your plan! Can we pray?

Lord, we invite you to influence our lives with your plan. We trust your wisdom and submit to your word. God, show us your way. Lord, show us your plan. Expand our scope in life; allow us to see into the provisions you have scheduled for our lives. Help us identify the people you have ordained connected to us. We thank you for what is already done, and we give you glory now. Amen!

Principles

- To experience success in life, marriage, ministry, business, or investments, a plan is necessary.
- God has a plan for our destiny.
- Failure to follow plans can have catastrophic results.
- God's plan is the equivalent of success.
- Sometimes yielding and surrendering to God's plan requires us to disconnect from our comfort zones.

Twelve

Take Your Foot Off the Brakes!

Take this for the journey:

We're the bridge across forever, arching above the sea, adventuring for our pleasure, living mysteries for the fun of it, choosing disasters, triumphs, challenges, impossible odds, testing ourselves over and again, learning love and love and LOVE!
~ Richard Bach, The Bridge across Forever ~

There is a destiny that makes us brothers –
None goes his way alone;
All that which we send into the lives of others,
Comes back onto our own.
~ Edwin Markham ~

The purpose of life, after all, is to live it, to taste experience to the utmost, to reach out eagerly and without fear for newer and richer experience.
~ Eleanor Roosevelt ~

I am extremely playful. I love to play jokes on my friends and family. One of my favorite pranks whenever I'm left in the car alone is to engage the emergency brake and watch, after the driver returns, as he or she shifts the car into reverse. I cackle inside as they panic because the car isn't moving. When I start to laugh, they realize I had something to do with it and interrogate me until the issue is resolved.

Many of us go through life with the brakes on. Negative thoughts control our perceptions. They affect the way we interact with other people and entertain opportunities. They also influence our ability to accept help. Take a minute to reflect:

- Negative thinking hinders you from sharing
- Negative thinking causes you to feel unworthy
- Negative thinking causes you to procrastinate
- Negative thinking causes you to fear
- Negative thinking causes you to second-guess your ability
- Negative thinking condenses your dream
- Negative thinking hinders your focus

I am surprised at the number of people who go through life with the brakes on. They make a conscience decision not to move beyond the realm of negativity. Negative thinking invites negative people into your life and negative outcomes in situations. Negative people thrive in stifling environments. Negative people create the atmosphere they expect. We all know people who change the atmosphere for the worse the moment they enter into a room. Their thoughts manifest through their behavior and infect everything they touch.

Negative people don't know how to enjoy the journey. The journey is a one-way street filled with one-dimensional realities such as denial, contradiction, disbelief, and protest. Their route hinders the trip. They enter the highway blinded by low expectations. They expect to be rejected, rather than accepted and welcomed.

> EXPECTING THE BEST MAY BE THE ANSWER TO RECEIVING IT

Don't miss your blessing by dwelling on negativity. "As a man thinketh in his heart so is he." Rather than predetermining outcomes based on past failures, embrace positive thought patterns. Expecting the best may be the answer to receiving it. We tend to get what we expect!

It is essential to foster and cultivate positive expectations. We can change what we get by changing our expectations. Wayne Dyer says, "Change your thoughts; change your life."

- Expect a yes!
- Expect promotion!
- Expect positive relationships!
- Expect more money!
- Expect greater opportunities!
- Expect doors to open for you!

Get off the brakes. You cannot go further until you move away from negativity and towards the incredible future waiting for you.

<u>Principles</u>

- Negative thoughts affect the way we interact with other people and entertain opportunities.
- Negative people create the atmosphere they expect.
- Rather than predetermining outcomes based on past failures, embrace positive thought patterns.
- Expecting the best may be the answer to receiving it.

THIRTEEN

DON'T FORGET YOUR KEYS

DAY 1

Be realistic!

Your goals must evolve with you. They should not be so simple that you can achieve them without effort or so difficult that they are completely out of reach. Keep your goals at a distance that keeps you trying, but in a position in which you will someday be able to reach them. Be realistic!

"For the Lord God will help me; therefore shall I not be confounded: therefore have I set my face like a flint, and I know that I shall not be ashamed." (Isaiah 50:7)

Daily declaration:

_____

_____

_____

_____

_____

_____

_____

_____

_____

_____

_____

_____

_____

_____

DAY 2

Confidence

Confidence is like a helpful virus spreading throughout your body. If you have it, it will infect everything you do in a positive way. If you don't, it will undermine everything you do. Confidence spreads with successes, and lack of confidence multiplies with failures. If your confidence falters, turn to what you do best and take on more challenging tasks.

"I can do all things through Christ which strengtheneth me." (Philippians 4:13)

Daily declaration:

_____

_____

_____

_____

_____

_____

_____

_____

_____

_____

_____

_____

_____

_____

DAY 3

Is it worth it?

Some problems can be avoided more easily than they can be eliminated, and some solutions are more costly than the problems they solve. In your efforts to be successful, the emphasis must be on winning with a purpose, not merely on winning. Trying to succeed in every single thing you do, winning every disagreement, and getting to do everything your way will lead you to a myopic focus on meaningless confrontations, instead of a big-picture focus on what you really want.

"What shall we then say to these things? If God be for us, who can be against us?" (Romans 8:31)

Daily declaration:

_____

_____

_____

_____

_____

_____

_____

_____

_____

_____

_____

_____

_____

_____

_____

_____

DAY 4

Refuse to be average.

Everywhere around you are average people. They entice you into being more like them by offering acceptance and leading you to believe that everyone else is already more like them than like you. But the "average person" sales pitch leaves out that you sacrifice your goals, individuality, and unique ideas, and that you will lead a life determined more by the preference of the group than by you.

"The Lord God is my strength, and he will make my feet like hinds' feet, and he will make me to walk upon mine high places. To the chief singer on my stringed instruments." (Habakkuk 3:19)

Daily declaration:

_____

_____

_____

_____

_____

_____

_____

_____

_____

_____

_____

_____

_____

_____

_____

_____

_____

_____

DAY 5

Keep moving.

People need to keep moving forward in order for their dreams to live. You do not need to do everything today, but you do need to do something every day.

"Though I walk in the midst of trouble, thou wilt revive me: thou shalt stretch forth thine hand against the wrath of mine enemies, and thy right hand shall save me." (Psalm 138:7)

Daily declaration:

_____

_____

_____

_____

_____

_____

_____

_____

_____

_____

_____

_____

_____

_____

_____

_____

DAY 6

Take a chance.

There is an element of chance in everything. Every aspect of your life has been affected by quirks of fate. Great jobs are found or ignored depending on who reads the classifieds that day. New opportunities are glimpsed or missed depending on who is paying attention. Still, you have to embrace the uncertainty of outcomes and realize that chance can play for you or against you on any given day, but the more you try, the greater your opportunity to benefit from an outcome.

"Thy word is a lamp unto my feet, and a light unto my path." (Psalm 119:105)

Daily declaration:

_____

_____

_____

_____

_____

_____

_____

_____

_____

_____

_____

_____
_____
_____

_____

DAY 7

Prepare yourself.

Take the first opportunity you have to get into the field of your dreams. Even if the job itself is not what you want, you will get a better idea of what that line of work entails, and you will begin to prepare yourself for the job you desire, or discover that it's not the right job for you and your plans need to be adjusted.

"Commit thy works unto the Lord, and thy thoughts shall be established." (Proverbs 16:3)

Daily declaration:

_____
_____
_____
_____
_____
_____
_____
_____

_____

_____

_____

_____

_____

_____

_____

_____

_____

DAY 8

Opposites attract.

There are starters and finishers. There are big-picture people and detailed people. Some are great at conceiving plans, but lose interest in following through on them, while others are tenacious in seeing a project through, but ill suited to dreaming up the next idea. You benefit when you involve people in your project who have traits and perspectives that are opposite yours.

"Love worketh no ill to his neighbor: therefore love is the fulfilling of the law." (Romans 13:10)

Daily declaration:

_____

_____

_____

DAY 9

Notice patterns.

What is the great common denominator of intellectual accomplishments? In math, science, economics, history, or any subject, the answer is the same—great thinkers notice patterns. They see patterns no one else has thought of, patterns no one else has paid attention to. Thinkers notice what goes along with what, and they consider the meaning behind those patterns. Take time to consider patterns in your world that you've never thought about before.

"The righteous shall flourish like the palm tree: he shall grow like a cedar in Lebanon." (Psalm 92:12)

Daily declaration:

_____

_____

_____

_____

_____

_____

_____

_____

_____

_____

_____

_____

_____

_____

_____

_____

<u>DAY 10</u>

Boredom is the enemy?

Boredom will eat away at your persistence and resolve. No one can do the same job, the same tasks, with perpetual interest and enthusiasm. When evaluating a job opportunity, don't just worry about the salary and workload—investigate how much variety there is in the tasks you'll perform.

"Submit yourself therefore to God. Resist the devil, and he will flee from you." (James 4:7)

Daily declaration:

_____

_____

_____

_____

_____

_____

_____

_____

_____

_____

_____

_____

_____

_____

_____

DAY 11

Don't be afraid to listen.

70

Nobody likes to be criticized. And to some extent, everyone displays some measure of defensiveness—the impulse to reject any and all criticisms by denying their validity or undermining the messenger. Unfortunately, defensiveness does not serve you. It encourages you to ignore potentially useful feedback, which inhibits your ability to improve. Know that you are capable, and show it. But do not fight criticism merely because you can.

"So then faith cometh by hearing, and hearing by the word of God." (Romans 10:17)

Daily declaration:

_____

_____

_____

_____

_____

_____

_____

_____

_____

_____

_____

_____

_____

_____

_____

_____

DAY 12

Winners are made, not born.

The great successes of our time are just extraordinary people on whom fate smiled, aren't they? No, in reality, they're not. Successful people get where they are by following a strategic plan. They learn what it takes to get ahead. We understand that to build a house it takes a plan, a blueprint—but we sometimes forget that a successful life needs a blueprint, too.

"Ye are the salt of the earth." (Matthew 5:13)

Daily declaration:

_____

_____

_____

_____

_____

_____

_____

_____

_____

_____

_____

_____

_____

_____

_____

DAY 13

Do things in order.

If you were making a sandwich, you would do it in order. First, a slice of bread, then the fillings and seasonings, then the other slice. It wouldn't make sense to change the order. Even if you really like mustard, you wouldn't put it on the plate first. When pursuing our goals, however, we see the steps we want to take and sometimes try to skip the steps that are less exciting, but stepping out of order is ultimately frustrating and futile. Take your goals one at a time and appreciate the process as you move forward. Otherwise, you won't.

"I will instruct thee and teach thee in the way which thou shalt go: I will guide thee with mine eye." (Psalm 32:8)

Daily declaration:

_____

_____

_____

_____

_____

_____

_____

_____

_____

73

_____
_____
_____
_____
_____
_____
_____
_____

DAY 14

Self-motivation works once.

"Declare something," say all the motivational speakers. What do you want? Declare that you shall have it. Want to be in better shape? Declare that you shall be. Want a better job? Declare that you shall have one. We are comforted, energized, and enthused by these declarations. Our mood, self-image, and self-esteem improve. Unfortunately, the effects are temporary and diminishing. When the outcome doesn't happen, we feel bad. And when we make our next declaration, it will be harder to work up even temporary enthusiasm as we recall the effects of our last failed plan. Success comes not from self-motivating tricks and declarations of desired outcomes, but from a steady, informed effort at progress.

"The steps of a good man are ordered by the Lord: and he delighteth in his way." (Psalm37:23)

Daily declaration:

_____

_____

_____

_____

_____

_____

_____

_____

_____

_____

_____

_____

_____

_____

_____

_____

_____

DAY 15

Where you stand depends on where you look.

Are you doing well? Average? Below average? We know the answer. It's obvious, isn't it? But how do you know the answer? Where does your response come from? These judgments, in truth, are entirely relative. Feelings of success are based on our position relative to those who have accomplished more.

Your feelings are as dependent on your frame of reference as they are on anything you've done.

"This people have I formed for myself; they shall shew forth my praise." (Isaiah 43:21)

Daily declaration:

_____

_____

_____

_____

_____

_____

_____

_____

_____

_____

_____

_____

_____

_____

_____

_____

_____

DAY 16

Negotiate with confidence, or don't.

You will face many negotiations in life, whether for a pay raise or the terms of a car purchase. What determines whether a negotiation is successful? Skill. Relative bargaining position. Ultimately, when negotiations are prolonged, your willingness to continue is based on your level of self-confidence. No matter what your other advantages might be, you will end negotiations faster if you lack confidence, which means you'll settle for a less advantageous resolution.

"If any of you lack wisdom, let him ask of God, that giveth to all men liberally, and upbraideth not; and it shall be given him." (James 1:5)

Daily declaration:

_____

_____

_____

_____

_____

_____

_____

_____

_____

_____

_____

_____

_____

_____

DAY 17

Volunteer to feel better.

You're busy. You don't feel there's much more you can do at work or home. But you want to do more and feel better doing it. Take an hour this week and volunteer. Yes, give your time away. Volunteering aids our community, but it also opens us to a greater appreciation of our own lives, which enhances our motivation to do what we do the best we can.

"Bear ye one another's burdens, and so fulfil the law of Christ." (Galations 6:2)

Daily declaration:

_____

_____

_____

_____

_____

_____

_____

_____

_____

_____

_____

_____

_____

_____

_____

_____

DAY 18

Efficiency in everything...

Every organization suffers some waste. We've heard stories of the federal government purchasing thousand-dollar hammers and hundred-dollar nails. Sometimes we laugh at these matters, but ultimately, they are very important. Nothing kills our initiative as quickly as the feeling that the organization will waste your resources or efforts.

"But my God shall supply all your need according to his riches in glory by Christ Jesus." (Philippians 4:19)

Daily declaration:

_____

_____

_____

_____

_____

_____

_____

_____

_____

_____

_____

_____

_____

_____

_____

<u>DAY 19</u>

Leadership is contagious.

True leadership strengthens followers. It is a process of teaching, setting an example, and empowering others. If you seek to lead, your ability will ultimately be measured in the successes of those around you.

"If they obey and serve him, they shall spend their days in prosperity, and their years in pleasures." (Colossians 4:1)

Daily declaration:

_____

_____

_____

_____

_____

_____

_____

_____

_____

_____

_____

_____

_____

_____

_____

_____

DAY 20

What is the point?

If you could pick one thing you most wanted out of your job and life, what would it be? While many of us chase money, prestige, and recognition, the single most important thing you can achieve is meaning. Having a purpose in everything you do makes every day valuable and every outcome, good or bad, worthwhile.

"But seek ye first the kingdom of God, and his righteousness; and all these things shall be added unto you." (Matthew 6:33)

Daily declaration:

_____

_____

_____
_____
_____
_____
_____
_____
_____
_____
_____
_____
_____
_____
_____
_____
_____

DAY 21

Success formula...

- Decide what you want. (Be precise! Clarity is power.)
- Take action. (Because desire is not enough)
- Notice what's working or not. (You don't want to expend energy on a worthless approach.)
- Change your approach until you achieve what you want. (Flexibility gives you power to create a new approach and a new result.)

Daily declaration:

_____

_____

_____

_____

_____

_____

_____

_____

_____

_____

_____

_____

_____

_____